# Rats live on no evil star

**Paul South**

Copyright © Paul South 2025
bigbillsblues@hotmail.com

This book is copyright. Apart from any fair deal for the purpose of private study, research, criticism or review, as permitted under the Copyright Act, no part may be reproduced by any process without written permission. Enquiries should be addressed to the author.

ISBN: 978-1-923216-91-4

Busybird Publishing

Text layout and book design by Initially NO
Cover concept by Paul South
Cover design by Gemma White
Cover redesign by Busybird Publishing

# ACKNOWLEDGEMENTS

Many of the rat poems have been previously published in *Roomers Magazine*. Also, "Toilet Phobia" was published on the audio anthology, *The CD side of Roomers*, which has received airplay on several radio stations including 3CR, Radio National and 3RRR.

"Things to do in Moreland", "AM Radio", "Blue train" and "Amber" have been published in podcast form on NMIT's on-line journal for the Bachelor of Writing and Publishing course. Also, several other pieces in this collection have appeared on episodes of *Red Lobster* on Channel 31. "Things to do in Moreland" is also currently being published in the literary journal, *Sacred/Profane*.

I wish to express thanks to all the gifted teachers and mentors who have helped me at different stages of this project. Among them are Andy Jackson, Matt Hetherington, Claire Gaskin, Stuart Reedy and Margaret McCarthy. Thanks also to Amanda Anastasi for her valuable help.

Special thanks to Bronwen Manger, Andy Jackson and Gemma White, for their patience, line edits and belief in my work. I wish to thank them for their unwavering friendship and support.

A final thanks goes to Initially NO for her work designing the book, and Gemma for making the cover concept a reality.

# Contents

### – SHORT TRIPS –

| | |
|---|---|
| AM radio | 11 |
| Songbird | 12 |
| Toilet phobia | 13 |
| Sleeping with a sore neck | 14 |
| Amber | 15 |
| Get used to it | 16 |
| Recovery | 17 |
| Real Estate | 18 |
| Transported | 19 |
| Dirge of myself | 20 |
| Dead crow | 21 |
| Walking laboratory | 22 |
| Garbage ideology | 23 |
| Sunset | 24 |
| Things to do in Moreland | 25 |
| I see the light | 26 |
| In my cage | 27 |
| Hurstbridge train | 28 |
| I am laughing with you | 29 |
| Blue train | 30 |
| Bat | 32 |

### – BRIDGE –

## – RATS LIVE ON NO EVIL STAR –

| | |
|---|---|
| I prefer the rats | 41 |
| What's a name | 43 |
| Fixed | 44 |
| Misunderstood | 45 |
| Right to the personals | 46 |
| A rat's diet | 47 |
| The love that dare not speak its name | 48 |
| The things I live with | 49 |
| Happy Xmas | 50 |
| Drums | 51 |
| Rescue rats | 52 |
| Utopia | 53 |
| March 22 | 54 |
| The rain | 55 |
| Rats live on no evil star | 56 |
| Metamorphosis | 57 |
| Graveside | 58 |

*For Gemma, for the journey*

# Short Trips

## AM radio

well
i've had my day out
walked a bit
seen some things
blobby trees
triangle ones
sweated
until the breeze
froze my nipples
drank coffee in the sun
wondered
and felt thankful
for the quiet
empty bus
that takes me
past flower beds
and lawns
as we turn and
turn again
on the drivers radio
cold chisel
singing
forever now

## Songbird

Eating is my life. Along with drinking coffee. I've been eating a pink jam doughnut for breakfast every second morning. The other mornings I make myself eat toast at home.

I sit in this cafe almost every day and drink a mug-o-chino, which is how they make them in Blackburn. The woman who owns the place is very familiar; she's like an Italian version of my mother, except she doesn't interfere in my life. I keep telling her that I'm going to stop coming there soon, because I can't afford it, but then I'm there again the next day or the day after that.

Sometimes when it's late I go for a walk through the parklands, and when I'm done I come back down Canterbury road and buy a chocolate sundae at the all-night McDonald's, and I get them to put the fudge underneath as well as on top. Then I eat it as I walk home. Then I watch Dave Letterman. Sometimes, when the brass and cheers on Letterman get me excited, I'll have another coffee.

I have Hep C, and last month I had an ultrasound done on my liver. The doctor told me I had a layer of fat around it. He said, what's your diet like? And I said, it's not the best. He suggested I consider replacing coffee with dandelion tea, and double-choc sundaes with apples. Alternatively, I might choose to go on Interferon.

Interferon has a tendency to cause some distress, he said, not to mention that it can make your hair fall out. However there was no hurry. In my case, the decision could wait a few years. Now there's a tune I can sing like a bird: *it can wait a few years.*

## Toilet phobia

I have a kind of phobia when sitting on the toilet that makes me look between my knees. I expect to see a hand coming out of the bowl, see it pulling my intestinal tract out of my arsehole and down around the u-bend, continuing until my kidneys and then my liver plops out into the bowl. I tell you, it's hard to do a shit when you think like this.

## Sleeping with a sore neck

walking around a blind house
paunched
smoking *Gitanes*
looking for a door
listening to a voice through the wall

sitting at a computer
in y-fronts
holding my neck

asking questions in an old friend's house
her daughter asks for a massage
too scared to say yes or no

a crook neck
some kind of find
in the crack
between dark and light

a vanilla cloud
secret radio coming through
all the dead are coming back
everything I never said
you too
come
say hello

## Amber

Your tears cannot
clear this matter from
your eyes.

She has gone,
left you blind and plodding,
like an insect
drowning in amber.

Now that she has gone
she rises
like an angel,
ablaze day and night.

You are almost hit
as you cross the street.

You are sure now:
all you want
is to be with her.

But she is above
and beyond;
she is everywhere,
so thin
and still.

You must continue on
going through the motions
inside a world
whose colour has changed.

## Get used to it

Struggled on the bus. Took liberties with the queue. Hey, it's an unfair world. Get used to it. Footscray is the unelected United Nations; they should know how it works.

I manage to get a seat that runs along the side of the bus. No room for my stuff. I dump everything on the floor, in the dirt, and cram it underneath. Now there's no room for my feet. A young Asian woman trips over my size 12. She turns to look at me. She is expressionless. "Sorry," I say as dispassionately as I can. She looks away again. Get used to it.

And you ought to be used to it by now, living in a pan-global sandwich, on this stupid bus, all elbows and mobile phones; throats hucking phlegm as we lurch forward. This is our life and this is how we share it; eyes that meet only in sly passing, none of us where we want to be.

## Recovery

Yeah, okay, sometimes
it's like a parasite
is eating away at me.
But it's not
the most significant thing
in my life anymore.

You can learn to…
no, that's not what I mean.
I mean,
you can live beyond
your demons.

It's not that they go away,
that they cease to exist;
it's just that you
live somewhere else.

They're like relatives.
You just
don't visit them
as much as you used to.

## Real Estate

I want to live
in an old weather-board
with an old bed
into which I can sink

with knitted blankets
heavy enough to pin me down
grey-water light
filtered through the lace

the lazy tune of a bird
traffic passing as a sigh
I want to become the musty smell
and permeate eternity

## Transported

A girl with short brown hair follows me on to the tram, wearing a brown and blue striped shirt. When she sits down, I think, *I reckon she's a lesbian*. She sits at a medium distance facing me, then moves to a nearer seat facing away. On closer inspection I decide that she isn't gay, or maybe she is but she mightn't be, and I think she moved closer to talk maybe. The tram starts to move and the sun flashes in my eyes.

I see us: we are lovers, the oldest of friends. We sit on the tram, holding hands. The young people look at us, wondering. We smile at them – a world-wizened, care-worn pair.

I'm looking at the back of her head, and her hair is a little too styled, too combed, a fraction too long. She's a straighty alright – the kind that is hung up, over-sensitive, a hypochondriac. The kind who wants a man to make her decisions for her, then blame him for not satisfying her in bed, for not being everything she ever fucking wanted.

I don't know this girl, I decide. She's alright, I guess.

## Dirge of myself

Ungainly, unemployed, you
dole out the moments,
saving yourself for that special day
when your body is somehow
more limber,
your movements freer;
when dawn is heartening
like a mug of mead,
when chi explodes out
of your crown chakra like ejaculate.

With Viking glint in your eye
and a thirty mile stare,
your giant blunnies crushing buildings
and smug suburban homes
in each stride,
you will turn the world beneath your feet.
And the world will relent:
the pope will step down and admit
he's just some bloke.
Howard will visit you personally
and apologise.

Oh, the great day.
And all you need do is wait.
Make another coffee
*– go on! –*
maybe write a haiku or two.
Patience is your virtue.
It must be great to be
such a martyr, a visionary.
Shithead.

## Dead crow

I was walking along in Footscray one day, and I found a dead crow next to a telephone pole. It was very hot so I kept on, but when I came back that evening he was still lying there, like a missing piece of jigsaw, right there on the nature-strip. He needed somewhere to rest. No-one was around, so I picked him up by the feet and dropped him in the garden of the nearest terrace-house.

I passed that way a few days later and I had a glance to see how he was doing. There was an Asian woman in the garden. She was staring at the crow, as if it were some kind of sign or omen; as if the Chinese mafia had put it there. She looked terrified.

I walked right past. I couldn't tell her, it's okay, it's only me; that I put him there because he needed some kind of dignity; that I wasn't a rapist, a murderer, a stalker; me with my unshaven face and white skin, a Footscray bum putting a decaying crow next to her geraniums.

## Walking laboratory

Frost-sequined stars,
car park rumours of rape
and torture, ecstasy
in the serotonin lights.
In every squealing tyre
the jaws of life.

I walk in the winter night
under sizzling towers,
beside identical cottages
in subdued hues
reaching for the moon.
Industry cries out
like beached whales
on the far shores of the sky.

I negotiate through shades
of black and grey.
I was born for the journey.
Want me to tell you who I am?
Am I
who I am?

I shrug off the cold like a coat
as I head inside
and close the door.

## Garbage ideology

I don't care how Zen it is
to make your own recycled paper,
knit your own jumpers,
or climb inside dumpsters to retrieve
other peoples junk:
*it will not save the world.*
I've tried it.
Did I save the world? No I didn't.
Did I cause a ripple effect? Not
that you could see in the moonlight.
Did people notice me in the *Savers* dumpster
at midnight,
waist-deep in wet clothes
and kids' toys?
Did it get back to the powers that be
that a change was in the air,
that a man
was gleaning
and that the world would have to re-think
its economic principles?

Of course it's hard to prove anything
for certain
in these uncertain times,
but lets hazard a little guess
and say
I don't think so.

## Sunset

what do I make of all this
air breathing me breathing
seagulls fragile as kites
flying slanted into the breeze

what do I make of me
climbing into the picture do I
make the sky and lake
the reflection of my eyes

where am I going leg
extended toward the world
stretching out
disappearing
in a perfect curve

and can this forward motion
be notated in words
and do the spaces
really make these words
so separate

do I make the slightest sound
with these shapes and
should I is it my place
the lake's glass surface
now split by a swan

## Things to do in Moreland

Buy umbrella from thrift shop.
Buy backpack from thrift shop.
Pick up dead pigeon.
Bury under the tree in Safeway car park.
Get egged by a car full of teenagers.
Write a poem about getting egged
       by a car full of teenagers.
Eat an over-ripe banana.
Stare at old Italian men staring at you.
Tell beggar you have no money.
Get dinged by a tram.
Meet Andy and bitch about poets.
Go to Brunswick Hotel
       and watch people get drunk.
Go to falafel joint at midnight
       and pack colon.
See Sydney Rd glazed in the wet.
Punch self in head
       just to feel something.
Clod along Merri Creek.
Piss behind the Willow tree.
Sniff fingers and look at the stars.

## I see the light

I was in a church op-shop looking at books
when I found the new testament
in a section marked "FICTION."
And I thought, wow,
this is my kind of church.

## In my cage

Life stands before me
like a huge gorilla
with a boner.

Every day I make a choice.
I can pull down my pants
and bend over,
or stand on my feet
and fight,
never to give up
while I'm still alive.

But for some reason
I am mesmerised
by life's enormity.
And anyway,
I've come to need
that big, black
gorilla cock in my arse,
reminding me
that I am a sick fuck
and giving me the punishment
that I deserve.

# Hurstbridge train

I know this line so well –
as if it were cut into the palm of my hand.

I know the morning glory at Montmorency,
the subdued skies of Ivanhoe.

The fading graffiti on tired fences;
I know it all.

The piddly creeks that wind through paddocks,
all winding up at Hurstbridge station.

When I got gang-bashed I always refused
to smudge my make up.

But you know, it didn't really happen here.
It happened in the '80s.

I close my eyes and see a man
bowling a cricket ball to his padded-up son.

I see oak trees,
the sun through the clouds.

The train screams through everything.
I begin to nod.

## *I am* laughing with *you*

Time stops forever.
Stop
with your watch!

Go.
Find God
under a rock.

Listen
until you are deaf

Ask why
until you fall asleep

Until you
never speaks again.

## Blue train

I'm on the train again, thinking
about the three kings, B.B., Albert and Freddy,
and how B.B. King is considered
*the king of kings*, although
Hendrix is more in the style of Albert.
Still, Jimi had the cheekiness
and some of the holler and reply of B.B.
Not that B.B. invented the holler
and reply. That goes way, way back…

There is a bad smell and a hissing sound.
When I look up I see a man with a silver face.
He is holding a plastic bag
that he is filling with paint from a can.
There's a wide circle of empty seats –
just a Chinese girl and I sit nearby;
everyone else is huddled up each end.

The guy is staring at me, like he wants
some kind of a reaction.
I look down, but a weird humour takes me.
When the Chinese girl notices me,
I smile and shake my head.
But she does not smile back.
I can't decide what her stony face means,
whether she is trying to tell me
that there is nothing funny about this,
or whether her lack of expression
is a cultural thing. Either way,
I feel shabby now – like I've shown this guy,
this sad person, a lack of respect.
I don't know what I'm supposed to do.
I guess humour is my defence.

I think about Tiananmen Square.
I think of Jimi Hendrix, and how he looked
not so young before he died.
Still this guy is staring at me
with his glazed eyes and silver-blue face,
sucking paint like there's no tomorrow.
Well maybe there is no tomorrow.

Sometimes the best I can do is the pension,
anti-depressants and self-restraint,
and to forgive myself for these visitations
of a humour that exists only to serve
its own blue world.

## Bat

I stand on a craggy rock.
I throw my voice
and catch just the end
bouncing back.

I write nothing,
reduce everything to a sound.
I've got nothing.
I make no apologies.

I stagger under the stars
like this, the world
in empty parenthesis,
a shadow-rat with my wings.

# Bridge

## Bridge

i

wake up in the
evening,
rats tickling me, trucks
passing.

i look in
the bathroom mirror,
and grin:
frightening!

oh well. slouch
down
on the toilet, head in
hands.

i'm trying not to
forget
something…

ii

washing my hands.
it's two a.m. and
i'm preparing for bed.

in the lather i see
people, friends
faces from years ago.

i'm happy to see them
though i know
we're not friends
anymore.

dig my nails into the soap.
i'm trying to get out
as much dirt and shit
as i can.

"i'm not saying i've
outgrown you,"
i say to the soap.


**iii**

i'm lying in bed
and starting to warm up,
when i remember
i haven't brushed my teeth.

it's an effort, but i can
make myself do things
a little
more these days.

i'm still dysfunctional
…i know.

**iv**

i work the bristles around
between my teeth
and spit out
toothpaste and blood.

i've got a bridge;
my front teeth aren't real.
i smashed
the real ones in.
i was riding a bicycle
stoned.

my parents bought the bridge
for my 30th birthday.
$5000.

i said, i'd prefer a car,
but they said
it wasn't up for discussion.
so i took the bridge.

"i'm no success story,
but i'm not so bad.
i could be worse," i say,

and my words
reverberate
around the bathroom.

**Rats live on no evil star**

## I prefer the rats

I open the window,
make coffee,
sit in my Jason *La-Z-Boy*.

There is a mid-morning lull:
the washing is already on and I've
changed the sheets.

I hear a couple of birds outside,
and the dull hum
of trucks and cars.

And I know, because I can feel it,
that there are six beady eyes
staring at me.

But the only thing I can smell
and the only thing I can think about
is rat shit.

The room is spotless, except
under the bed
and that, I guess, explains it.

My room. I remember one time
I went to call it my rats' cage.
As in, *I'll just nip back into my rats'* –

That's one hell of a Freudian slip.

But it doesn't really smell like a rat's cage.
It smells more like
a gorilla's enclosure.

And while I sit in this stink,
I think of my mum
and other women I know too,
saying:

*You'll never get a girlfriend with those rats, you know, your room smells like a cattle shed! How do you expect to catch a woman like that? How do you ever expect to get a girlfriend with rats in your bed? No wonder you don't have a girlfriend, girlfriend, girlfriend...*

Well let me set the record straight:

Firstly, I am not trying to catch a woman.
For all the connotations,
I'm not fly-fishing and a woman is not a trout.

And secondly, my room
does not smell like a cattle shed.
It smells like a gorilla's enclosure.

And if you want to talk about my rats,
feel free to come around
and talk to them any time.

They'll probably listen to you more than I will –
because frankly my dears, I don't give a rats!

## What's a name

I don't name my rats. I let them name themselves. It's no big deal. Some of them never have a name. And really, why should they? What I love about them is that they are <u>not human</u>. So why would I want to name them George, or Frank, or Bush Junior? Why would I name them Nylex, or Sprocket? I hate brand names, objects. I hate everything.

I don't name rats; I let them name themselves. But really, if they had no names at all, I wouldn't care. And why should they have names? After all, that is precisely why I love them – because they're <u>not human</u>. Why should I name them Silvagni, or Boccaccio, or Lollapalooza? They don't care. Why call them Palindrome, Jonestown, or Flintoff? It's all just stuff. And stuff sucks.

I've never named my rats. The names just came down the track. I don't think it really matters, does it? I named one Generic, but it didn't take. I named one Vermin. I was trying to be clever. There's no point being clever with a rat; they're operating on a higher level – sensitive, manic, soft, tyrannical, paranoid, gentle, sleepy, warm.

I don't name my rats, but they name themselves sometimes – like, say, a year down the track. It really is a pointless exercise; they have no idea what I'm saying. It's just something that happens because I happen to be a human, and humans want to know who they are talking to.

I don't name my rats, but then again I guess I do. What I mean is, rats don't speak the way that you or I do. I suppose you might say that I am speaking for them. But their names do come in basic, everyday ways. Here are some of their names: Brownie, Whitey, Biggie, Enigma and the one whose name is whatever I call him. One day it's honey, or sweetie, or you little shit; next day it's just hey, you.

## Fixed

It made no difference. And when I say no, I mean
none, nil, nix. Three rats – six hundred bucks.
Exactly whose balls were cut off again?
They called it a special rate. Six hundred bucks
is cheap, they said. They are taking it
in direct debits out of my dole.
I'll be living on beans and bread forever,
just like my boys. And to make it worse

I hear them committing atrocities on each other;
every scuffle and frantic squeak.
Then in the morning when I look under the couch
it's *Helter Skelter*, *Repulsion*.
I find all these scabby holes in my ratties
where nice soft fur should be.
I don't understand it: they are so gentle with me.

No, nothing is fixed.
I think that they are teaching me this.
My room is a laboratory.
We are a study in animal behaviour.
Hand to mouth, I am learning
the painful truth.

## Misunderstood

I went into this bargain shop in Footscray
and an Indian man came up to me.
I asked him if he had any rat cages.
He thought for a second,
then led me down an aisle
and pointed to a box marked
RAT POISON.

I told him, no, I don't want to *kill* the rats;
I want to *house and feed them*.
But I don't think he understood.

# Right to the personals

I want to be understood.
I want to be loved.
I want people in my life
who understand why I love rats.

And sometimes
I forget the order of things.

I sit next to an attractive
woman
(a nice girl, a well-cared-for
older woman, easy-going,
maybe a little bit hippy)
on the train and
pull a rat out of my bag.

I may as well pull out my cock.

Once I had an ad in The Age
personals page, saying:

LOVE ME, LOVE MY RATS.
WRITER SEEKS
LIKE-MINDED SOUL.

No-one replied.
It was in there for months.

What can I say? I get it. I can
take a fucking hint.
Children are sacrosanct
and rats are just giant cockroaches,
furry pieces of shit.

Whatever. Good on you,
womankind.

# A rat's diet

People often ask me*, they say, "Paul, what do rats eat?" Well biologically speaking, they need all sorts of grains, roots and grasses, and of course fruits and vegetables. A rat's diet really is a thing of science. It's a side-effect of them being used in laboratories for so long: scientists have all but perfected their diet in pellet-form. But that is just theoretical.

Rats eat anything. And what they can't, well it's not from a lack of trying. I've seen mortifying turds – I mean, it's hard to believe these things came from a living organism.

Sometimes when I'm in bed they sink their fangs into my pinkies. Not to the point of drawing blood; just a pinch. Then when I flinch or go "Ow!" they run away. They can't quite accept that my toes are attached to the rest of me. I think it's a kind of wishful thinking. Not that I would want it any other way: if I should die before my time, I hope that my rats will consider me an all-you-can-eat buffet.

*No-one has ever actually asked me this.

## The love that dare not speak its name

Admit it. Reading this book you have considered the homo-beastio-erotic possibilities between me and my rats. It's human nature: the nuns and the candle-sticks, all that flicking of wet towels in the locker-rooms, and the connotations of gerbils, just because they are roughly the same size as you-know-what.

Well if it gives you some pleasure to picture me with a rat lodged in my lower intestine, why not, go ahead – knock yourselves out. But the truth is far less racy. My boys are neutered, for one thing – and courtesy of anti-depressants I'm not far behind. Besides, we're just not into each other in that way. Not that there haven't been encounters of a sort.

In the winter months I used to let them climb into my bed, but I was forever kicking them, and yes, they'd tickle and sniff me, and while it didn't turn me on, it was a little too intimate. If by chance I were to wake up in the middle of the night and "find myself", I would almost inevitably just be getting somewhere when these whiskers would tickle my leg and I'd leap about a foot off the bed.

Our sleeping arrangements reached a painful climax in the wee hours of a dark winter's night, when a rat sank his fangs into my knob-end. I think he mistook it for a giant chick-pea. I never knew who it was, but I suspect Biggie, because he always was a hungry boy. Anyway, they all got relocated to the lounge-room after that.

I'm happy to tell you that my knob did not go green and drop off, but like I said, I wonder if I'd even notice sometimes. So anyway, it's back to the lone ranger; just me and my one-eyed side-kick in the sack. There you go; the air is hereby cleared. Bachelor equilibrium is restored.

## The things I live with

They stick their nose in everything. They are all nose – it's the thin end
of the wedge. They
eat the buttons off my remotes,
crap in my dirty clothes pile,
go to sleep in the middle of my book.
But their master-stroke came when I was going for a job interview; my
first one in a year.

I remember that day clearly. The early morning sun streamed in;
September birds flitted past the window. I showered, brushed my teeth,
flossed. I trimmed my nails; ironed my resume. Then I went to the
cupboard to get my suit out.

I bought this suit about 6 months earlier but hadn't worn it yet because
nobody had died and, as I said, I wasn't big in the job-hunting way.
Okay, so you have to imagine me in my socks and jocks. I open the
cupboard. The suit is there. It's hard to see it that well because it's dark
in there and the suit is black, but already I have a bad feeling.

I pull the suit out. The suit is layered in a toxic slick of urine and fur.
The front of it, and the back too when I turn it over, has hundreds of
holes in it. I couldn't believe that my rats did it at first – it looked like
giant moths had hatched in it. It was decimated. Like my job prospects.

Now I don't mean to say that I blame the rats – after all, I was the one
who put the boxes in the bottom of the cupboard, making a step-ladder
up to my suit – but at that moment its true that I had pretty much lost my
sense of humour. I scooped them up in one quick movement. Visions of
squeezing them like soft-toys flared before my eyes. But up close and
personal with a rat, well, what is there to say?

My rats are old now, and they don't fang it quite as much as they used
to, but they can still be a plague on any given day. And hey, I can live
with that. It's a price I'm willing to pay.

## Happy Xmas

My rat smells like Xmas cake
and that's because
I gave him some.

## Drums

One night when it was very late
and Footscray was as quiet as it can be,
Whitey climbed up on the bed.

He licked my forehead and then
groomed my hair. After a while,
he laid down upon my ear.

I heard his little heart.
It must have been
a thousand beats to the minute.

How incredible is this tiny heart
beating like this for two years, even three.
That is the miracle.

And when he finally moved off,
I was left there feeling
that he was still upon my ear

as I lay listening to the distant steel
sounds of Coode Island;
the machinery of the city's dreams.

## Rescue rats

I was given them as a gesture of good faith; from one dual diagnosis patient to another. A friend of mine had committed suicide, and at the time, I wanted to justify her death. At the funeral I said, "She fought hard, harder than any of us. She is better off this way. She has earned her rest."

I don't know. It was some time around then, anyway. I was changing anti-depressants for the third time in a year, and nothing seemed quite real. At night I would walk until the first bird. I'd look at the trees, all the humble, cared-for front yards, and cry. I really don't know why. During the days I sweated. Everything seemed to be made of plasticine. At sunset the crickets would ring out like so many unanswered phones.

Then one day it occurred to me, as if it were the first thought I'd ever had, that maybe I was better off dead too. I couldn't take such a thought seriously; I just dismissed it. But the thought returned, and again, and each time it came as a muddled surprise. Example: I'd be waiting for the kettle to boil, and something in that grey steam would tell me it was time to leave. And each time I heard this, it seemed more certain than before. It felt like relief – as if I were already dead, and, being dead, I had no reason to fear life anymore.

Well, then came the rats. I had talked about rats, made a few noises, but then one day they just landed clear out of the sky: two rats, straight up. Right in my lap. I cursed them; I cursed the day I got them. I wasn't sure I could keep them: they demanded so much of my attention. They were busy and always on the make. Like beggars in Delhi. Just at me, all the time.

You've got to laugh, really. Those annoying little shits saved me. Two quicksilver segues into today, all over me like a rash, marking me with their scent, shitting in my bed, forcing me to wash my sheets and shower every day. More feral even than me.

## Utopia

My utopia is in the mountains somewhere. I will have a log cabin, and my rats can go outside and play. I'll sing snippets of songs my grandmother used to sing, and wear an apron as I stoke up the wood-fire stove. Then when the sun dims between the trees, I'll call my ratties home, and they'll come running to my arms. We'll eat to our hearts' content, then doze in front of the fire, all warm and snoring and furry.

# March 22

My Brownie is not who he once was – his spirit, his life force is leaving him, day by day. But he loves me as much as ever. Sometimes he will sleep under my chin for hours, too tired to worry about his space; then when I go to pick him up he lets out a squeak he never used to. He can't see and has trouble walking, so no wonder he gets afraid.

Sometimes I get afraid. Then I relax when I look at him: he is not afraid, not generally, anyway. He is old, that's all. He sleeps a lot, nearly all day and night. One day soon his body will sleep forever, and I think his body will be grateful for this. I think all bodies are happy when their time finally comes.

## The rain


wake from a dream,
perhaps half a dream:
it seems
you are here

i hear your pattering feet

but you know, it's just
the rain
falling like angels,
like
stars

## Rats live on no evil star

*Now all us cursed ones falling out after*
*... do not go to some heaven, some hell*
*but are put on the RAT'S STAR.*
                    – Anne Sexton

I have lived with them –
an endless procession of visitations,
each one shadowing the before
and after. And they are
visitations – a thing glimpsed
from the periphery of your vision,
real shooting stars.

If we descend from angels
they are from the line of pixies,
fairies and wood-sprites.
Mischief is theirs by nature –
they do run-throughs
when I'm in the shower;
they plunder my back-pack.

I lost my last twenty dollars
and when I lifted up the lounge,
there it was – with three rats
sleeping on it.

It's the fading of this magic
that is hard to accept.

Yet even in death I find them –
they tickle my leg, rustle the papers,
I find them in my sock-pile
as possibility. I'm careful where I step
because they are never far from here,
watching, quietly waiting.

## Metamorphosis

I am the rat these days, inspecting this, having a nibble of that.
Disguised as a human, I go to work.
"How are you?" says my boss.
"Fine," I say.
I have learned the turns of speech, digested talk of news, sport and
weather. Rats have strong stomachs, and are very adaptable. But a rat
never forgets his place in the food-chain. The hand that feeds can also kill.

Sometimes I step into a trap. My boss's huge face looms around
the corner, says "What are you doing?" and I'm caught there in the
spotlight, a crumb still hanging from my mouth. I try to speak, but all
that comes out is a muffled squeak! My body goes limp, as if dead –
I think I am dead – then after a while she goes off again.

Then I go home, to the dark little corner of my world. It's nothing special,
but it's my dark corner, and I am quite happy with it thank you! But even
then my mind play tricks on me; I hear things, a footstep, a word. I am
never really alone: I'm always being chased by things that I cannot see or
name. And there is no hiding from the fact that, sooner or later, I will have
to go out there again, into the open. I have to if I am going to survive.

My poor heart! I scurry about right under their noses, filling shelves,
collecting trolleys. This check out chick keeps checking me out. I squeak
a few words. I don't know what to do. I keep thinking, they'll see me –
they'll see the light reflect off my eyes and know me for what I am.
But they never do.

Time moves on. I get so caught up in what I am doing that I forget what
I am, and then I find myself being patted by somebody. I look up and
wonder how it is that I am here, that I am not afraid, here in the palm of
a human's hand.

## Graveside

I want to make things happen now,
to feel it, know it's true;
falling from the sky,
a life, my life.

Pin up the sequin stars.
Call all the gods into orbit.
Sit under the singing rat tree,
the choir of crickets,
the chimney-smoke, me.